P9-ARI-687

# UFOs

by Judith Herbst

L Lerner Publications Company • Minneapolis

HARFORD COUNTY
PUBLIC LIBRARY
100 E. Pennsylvania Avenue
Bel Air, MD 21014

3 1526 02768049 2

Copyright © 2005 by Judith Herbst

All rights reserved. International copyright secured. No part of this book may be
reproduced, stored in a retrieval system, or transmitted in any form or by any means—
electronic, mechanical, photocopying, recording, or otherwise—without the prior written
permission of Lerner Publications Company, except for the inclusion of brief quotations
in an acknowledged review.

Lerner Publications Company
A division of Lerner Publishing Group
241 First Avenue North
Minneapolis, Minnesota 55401 U.S.A.

Website address: www.lernerbooks.com


Library of Congress Cataloging-in-Publication Data

Herbst, Judith.
        UFOs / by Judith Herbst.
           p.    cm. — (The unexplained)
        Includes index.
        Summary: Investigates several well-known accounts of UFO sightings as well as
    theories aimed at explaining why such reports cannot be true.
        ISBN: 0-8225-0961-X (lib. bdg. : alk. paper)
        1. Unidentified flying objects—Juvenile literature.  [1. Unidentified flying objects.]
    I. Title.  II. Unexplained (Lerner Publications)
    TL789.2.H49  2005
    001.942—dc22                                                    2003015806

Manufactured in the United States of America
1 2 3 4 5 6 – JR – 10 09 08 07 06 05

WITHDRAWN

OCT 3AAG

OCT 2005

# Table of Contents

Something
is seen,
but one doesn't
know what.

—Carl Jung

4

# MARS ATTACKS

We have been dreaming about Mars for a long, long time. We have imagined crystal cities rising out of the red Martian sand. We have heard water rushing through the dry riverbeds. We have seen the Martian canals. A Martian breeze has touched our faces. And in our hearts we always knew we would meet them someday. They would come to our planet. The Martians.

It began in the 1700s, when astronomers turned their telescopes toward Mars and saw great wonders. There were two icy polar caps, just like on Earth. There were seasonal color changes, as

Astronomer William Herschel constructed this large reflecting telescope to observe the night sky. A complex of scaffolding supports the weight of the telescope.

if winter were giving way to a blooming spring. There were bright, white patches. "Clouds," whispered the English astronomer William Herschel. "Those must be clouds." And where there were clouds, there would be water. So by the 1800s, everyone simply assumed this planet that was so much like Earth would also have life.

Night after night, the astronomers struggled to sketch the face of Mars. But the atmosphere often trembled, and Martian dust storms blocked their view. A full moon rose and washed away the tiny planet in a blaze of light. Tantalized more than ever, the astronomers pushed on. Close-up photographs of the Martian surface were still one hundred years in the future. So with hard, sharp pencils the astronomers copied the faint lines they saw, each working alone in the starry night.

In 1840 two German astronomers at last published the first global map of Mars. But they had no idea what they were looking at. Mars didn't really have any familiar features. There were no mountains or lakes or deep canyons—only white patches and dark, shadowy smears. But the two astronomers gave everything a name anyway. They called the dark areas oceans and seas. The lighter areas became continents.

It so happened that in Italy, astronomer Pietro Secchi had managed to make out some faint streaks on the planet's surface. Secchi didn't know what he was looking at either. So he decided to follow the custom and call the lines he saw *canali.* Of course, Secchi was speaking Italian, and in Italian the word *canali* is not what it sounds like in English. Canali

## WHAT DID YOU BRING ME?

NASA plans to search for signs of Martian life include the Sample Return Lander, scheduled to leave Earth in October 2011. The most sophisticated space robot ever, the Lander will spend four months on the Red Planet, gathering souvenirs. In December 2012 it will launch itself, returning home with its booty nine months later. And if any Martian life wants to stow away, that would be just lovely.

At one time, astronomers were convinced that the light and dark areas they saw on Mars were continents and oceans. This map of Mars from the 1800s shows the names scientists gave to areas of land and water, such as Herschel Continent and Dawes Ocean.

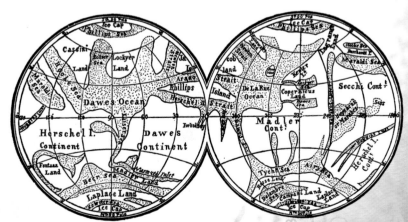

are channels, or naturally forming streambeds. But English-speaking astronomers must not have had their Italian/English dictionaries handy because what they heard was "canals," and canals are another story. Canals are artificial waterways. They are something that people build. So if Mars had canals, then it must also have . . . Martians? Oh, my!

Astronomers everywhere raced to their telescopes, anxious to see the canals for themselves. In America, William Pickering even added "oases" to the picture, which he said he saw where sections of the canals were joined to each other. But at the Lick Observatory in California, Edward Barnard just shrugged. Barnard was known to be a whiz at the telescope. He had sharp eyes and a lot of patience. But try as he did, Barnard could not make out one single canal. Lines? Oh, sure, there were plenty of lines. But lines were not waterways. A skeptical Barnard remained unconvinced.

The air, however, was crackling with Martian mania. Plans were even under way to try to signal the Martians. But nobody was more feverish with excitement than the American astronomer Percival Lowell. Lowell was so in love with

Percival Lowell (1855–1916) devoted much of his life to observing Mars. He built an observatory in Flagstaff, Arizona, to aid in his search for life on Mars.

A map of Mars drawn by Lowell in 1896 shows a network of canals and oases crossing the surface. In Lowell's opinion, canals on Mars could mean only one thing—someone or something had to have built them!

Mars that he had dipped into the family fortune and built an entire observatory just so he could study the planet. So when he heard that canali had been discovered, he almost fell off his chair. (Obviously he didn't have an Italian/English dictionary either.) Out he went into the icy night, prepared to freeze his pantaloons off if necessary for a few good peeks. This would have been fine had Lowell kept his imagination in check. But the thing got the better of him, and Lowell began to fantasize.

Mars, he said, was dying. The water that had once flowed so freely was drying up. The planet was becoming a desert, whose red sands would blow and shift as the Martian winds howled across space. Alas, the polar caps were all that remained. And so those brave little aliens had built a great system of canals to bring the water down from the poles to nourish the thirsty inhabitants.

"Henderson," he called, "you saw that shooting star last night?"

"Well?" said Henderson.

"It's out on Horsell Common now."

"Good Lord!" said Henderson. "Fallen meteorite! That's good."

"But it's something more than a meteorite. It's a cylinder—an artificial cylinder, man! And there's something inside!"

—H. G. Wells,
*The War of the Worlds*

Lowell was so moved by his own sad story, he wrote a number of books describing the Martian woes. All the books were fiction, of course, but Lowell didn't think about that, and neither did his readers. His fantasies sold like hotcakes to a public that had come to believe in Martians. But the Martians turned ugly in 1898, when English author H. G. Wells published his great science fiction story, *The War of the Worlds.*

Wells's Martians were more insectlike than human and bent on destruction. They arrived in metallic cylinders with a plan to colonize Earth. Armed

A film still from the 1953 movie based on H. G. Wells's *The War of the Worlds.* More than fifty years after the book was published in 1898, it still captured people's imaginations.

One of the earliest known photographs of an unexplained flying object (UFO) was taken on July 27, 1907, over Drobak, Norway. The UFO hovers in the sky above two sailing ships.

with death rays, the Martians blasted everything in sight and seemed to have the upper hand—or rather, tentacle. But their alien chemistry was no match for earthly bacteria, which eventually killed them off.

*The War of the Worlds* was wildly popular. But when the century turned, Wells would see his story become even more spectacular.

## >> Halloween Hysterics

Sightings of UFOs, or unexplained flying objects, go back quite some time. In 1917 a Pennsylvania teenager claimed to have seen a saucer-shaped object with rows of lights. In 1922 a high-pitched sound caught the attention of William Lamb of Hubbell, Nebraska. Moments later, Lamb watched a bright, circular object slowly land in a small valley. Sightings were being reported from every continent, and this quietly fueled the

Orson Welles broadcasts H. G. Wells's tale *The War of the Worlds* on October 30, 1938.

Martian madness. Then, on the evening of October 30, 1938, Orson Welles dished up a whopper of an invasion scare that people still talk about to this day.

It was a Sunday, the night before Halloween. Thousands of people had their radios tuned to the Columbia Broadcasting System's *Mercury Theatre on the Air* presentation. Orson Welles, the show's director, had planned a special scary treat for his listeners. At 8:00 P.M. sharp, the *Mercury Theatre* theme music rose and fell, and Welles addressed the audience in a serious tone.

"We know now," he said, "that in the early years of the twentieth century this world was being watched closely by intelligences greater than man's. . . . " Listeners were riveted.

Welles set the stage. We were being studied, he said. As humans went about their business, somewhere *out there* plans were being made.

The program cut to an announcer giving the weather report. Next came a supposedly live broadcast of dance music from the Meridian Room in the Park Plaza Hotel. And then Welles broke in. "Ladies and gentlemen, we interrupt our program of dance music to bring you a special bulletin from the Intercontinental Radio News."

And so it began. Orson Welles had taken H. G. Wells's classic story *The War of the Worlds* and turned it into a fake news broadcast. The Martians, it seemed, had landed in New Jersey and were blasting everything in sight with their ray guns. Earth was in big-time trouble. And the audience heard it all as it was happening. That's what they thought, anyway, and they really panicked.

As the actors in the broadcast booth calmly read their lines, screaming people were filling the streets. Police stations were swamped with calls. Roads were jammed. People prayed in Virginia. Five college students fainted in North Carolina. In San Francisco, volunteers lined up to fight the Martian invaders. And in Pittsburgh, one woman was actually about to take poison when her husband came home just in time.

Wild? It was very wild. Welles later admitted that he was shocked by the reaction. But the listeners had been primed. Even before Secchi's canali announcement, respected astronomers had talked about life on Mars. UFOs were being seen. Hollywood was making movies about rubbery space monsters and trips to the moon. Even the U.S. government was beginning to wonder. The public simply became caught up in the madness. And it would only get loonier.

# AND SO IT BEGINS. . . .

Kenneth Arnold was not seeking publicity, but he sure got it. Big time. At about three o'clock on a June afternoon in 1947, Arnold spotted something a little weird through the window of his plane. He was headed southeast over the Cascade Mountains, on his way to Yakima, Washington. Suddenly he saw. . . . Actually, he wasn't really sure what he saw. Nine objects, he said, flying at a fantastic speed. They were, maybe, 10,000 feet up. Arnold watched with mounting curiosity as the objects dipped in and out of formation. Hmmm. Strange.

Arnold landed in Yakima, casually mentioned the event to a few people, and took off again. But when he arrived at Pendleton, Oregon, the reporters were waiting.

"Mr. Arnold! Mr. Arnold! What did you see up there?"

Arnold was mobbed. He was also somewhat puzzled. He had decided that the crescent-shaped objects had been secret military aircraft. After all, what else could they be? But Arnold patiently described his sighting to the press. He even drew a little picture for them. "They moved," he said, "like a saucer skipping across the water."

Kenneth Arnold (shown here with camera and on facing page with UFO drawing) reported seeing strange objects flying through the sky during a flight over the Cascade Mountains of the Pacific Northwest.

"A saucer!" screamed the press. "You mean a *flying saucer*?"

"No," said Arnold. "They were crescents. Look, here, in my drawing...."

But the reporters paid no attention, and that's how the term *flying saucer* was born.

## >> The Government Gets into the UFO Business

We still don't know what Kenneth Arnold saw in the clear Washington skies that day. Some have said it was a flock of birds. Others believe it was just airplanes. Still others think Arnold had been fooled by an optical illusion. But those nine bright objects sure caught the attention of the government.

One year after Arnold's sighting, *Fate* magazine published this cover illustration of Arnold's encounter with what many people believe to have been flying saucers.

## MR. SMITH AND MR. JONES

Part legend and part something else, the so-called Men in Black have been popping up since the 1950s. It is said that those who get too close to the "truth" about flying saucers are apt to be visited by two or three men in black suits, white shirts, black ties, and homburg hats. Men in Black are mysterious, move like robots, and warn witnesses to keep their mouths shut—or else! You gotta love it.

Actually, the government had been troubled by reports of unidentified flying objects even before the Arnold sighting. If something's sneaking around up there and it's not ours, the government said, we sure as shootin' want to know about it! So in 1948 they organized Project Sign.

Project Sign's mission was pretty straightforward: find out what all those unidentified flying objects are and write a report. But after a year of study, the investigators knew about as much as they did on the day they began—nothing. All they had managed to do was group the UFOs into four categories. These things were either flying disks, cigar-shaped bodies, spheres, or balls of light that could climb, change direction, and reach very high speeds.

Well, that's all very interesting, but what *were* they?

The authors of Project Sign had to admit they didn't know. It seems, they said, that whoever is building these aircraft is technically way ahead of the United States. Maybe it's the

17

Astronomer Clyde Tombaugh, who discovered the planet Pluto, reported seeing pale yellow lights moving across the sky above Las Cruces, New Mexico, on August 20, 1949. Tombaugh couldn't explain his sighting. At right is an artist's interpretation of the event.

Soviet Union, they suggested. But they didn't think that was possible.

All right, then. Who?

Uh . . . the UFOs, said the authors of Project Sign, might be "aerial visitors from another planet."

This kind of talk scared everyone, so that was the end of Project Sign. It was not, however, the end of the sightings, which were numbering in the hundreds. Like a mosquito that keeps buzzing around your head, UFOs continued to appear. So in 1949, the government launched Project Grudge.

Okay, said the members of Project Grudge a year later. We studied the situation, and we have to tell you that these UFOs are a whole lot of nothing. They are not super-duper advanced flying machines. There are no aliens inside them, and they did not come from another planet. In fact, a big chunk of the sightings are mistakes. You know, people see the planet Venus. It's very bright, and they think it's a UFO. And, of course, a lot of the reports are hoaxes. People are fibbing, making up stories. The rest are hallucinations. Nut cases. Thank you very much. This concludes our report.

It's hard to say if the government was relieved. Probably not, because the UFOs didn't look like they had any intention of going away. If anything, their magic act became even more maddening. "So we don't exist, do we?" they seemed to be saying. "Get a load of this!" And in September 1951, a UFO showed up on army radar, of all places. The object was spotted on radar at Fort Monmouth, New Jersey. It was moving so fast, the air traffic controller couldn't even track it. In a 48-hour period, a total of four UFOs were picked up on radar. And when the pilot of a T-33 jet reported

This photograph was taken in July 1952 over New York City. While some UFO sightings have proven to be hoaxes and some can be explained by natural phenomena, there are other sightings that remain mysteries.

The staff of Project Blue Book stands behind Major Hector Quintanilla Jr. Of a total of 12,618 sightings reported to Project Blue Book between 1947 and 1969, 701 remain unidentified.

seeing an unidentified object some 30 to 50 feet in diameter, everybody agreed that this sort of thing could not be allowed to continue. So the government called back Project Grudge, changed its name to Project Blue Book, and demanded that it identify the UFOs.

## >> Does Radar Lie?

For whatever reason, things became very lively in the summer of 1952. Just before midnight on July 19, eight UFOs appeared over the Capitol in Washington, D.C. Witnesses—and there were plenty of them—said the objects zipped this way and that, changing direction with amazing speed. Since it was dark, no one actually saw any disks—only lights. But there sure must have been something solid in the sky, because it all showed up very clearly on radar.

Harry Barnes was the area's chief air traffic controller at the time, and he immediately gave the order to send a squadron of air force jets to intercept the . . . uh . . . lights. But the jets had to come from a base in Wilmington, Delaware. And—you guessed it—by the time the jets arrived, the lights were gone. So the jets headed back to Wilmington, but as soon as they left Washington, the lights were back. Playing a game of cat and mouse, perhaps?

The government didn't think any of this was funny, and it became even less funny when the UFOs showed up again one week later. From 9:00 P.M. until 2:00 A.M., radar tracked as many as 12 UFOs, all silently dancing over the Capitol dome. So again air force jets were scrambled, and again the UFOs disappeared just in the nick of time. Back went the jets to Wilmington. Back came the UFOs.

At 3:00 A.M., another squadron of jets was sent to Washington, but this time the UFOs hung around, and pilot Lieutenant William Patterson spotted them. "I can see the lights," he reported. "They're bluish-white and tremendous. Tremendous!"

## EARTH VERSUS THE FLYING SAUCERS

The Washington UFO flap was a dream come true for Hollywood. In 1956 special effects master Ray Harryhausen buzzed his way into movie theaters with Earth versus the Flying Saucers. In the movie, the aliens were eventually shot out of the sky by an anti-flying-saucer death ray, which saved the day but totally wrecked Washington. The smoldering flying saucer sticking out of the Capitol dome was a particularly nice touch.

21

The air traffic controllers back on the ground could hardly believe what they were hearing.

"They're just ahead of me," said Patterson, "in a kind of cluster. I'm approaching."

And then, "They've formed a ring around me." Patterson's voice was shaking. "What should I do?"

The controllers were speechless. But if they had a good idea up their sleeves, Patterson would never hear about it. Seconds later, the UFO circle broke up, and Patterson found himself alone in the sky.

The Washington sightings had so many eyewitnesses that there was no way government officials could ignore what had happened. They had to say something. So on July 29 they held a press conference. They announced that the unknown targets observed over Washington were the result of a temperature inversion.

Of course, that was silly, and the government knew it. A temperature inversion is just a layer of air in which the temperature increases rather than decreases with height. But they must have thought it was better to sound silly than ignorant.

The CIA put together a panel to investigate the situation. Maybe a bunch of scientists could figure it all out. But the scientists weren't really interested in UFOs, and they made rather fast work of it. UFOs are known objects, they said. There's no threat to national security (even though the UFOs had entered restricted airspace when they flew over the Capitol). There aren't any aliens. And we strongly recommend that future UFO reports be dismissed as nonsense. The public is getting too worked up over this.

This UFO was photographed by George J. Stock in Passaic, New Jersey, on July 19, 1952.

When Project Blue Book came to the same conclusions, astronomer J. Allen Hynek fired off a letter to the Office of the Secretary of the Air Force. Hynek was troubled. I think you have to turn this problem over to a panel of civilian scientists, he said. Somebody has to review the findings of Project Blue Book.

The air force actually agreed to this, probably because they were sick of the whole UFO thing. So in 1966, the University of Colorado signed a contract with the air force to investigate UFO reports. Unfortunately, the Colorado Project, as it was called, got nowhere. In fact, we're still bumping around in the dark. Over the years, there have been thousands and thousands of sightings. Most can be explained. But some can't. The UFOs' radar tracks are real. The photos people take of them are real. The marks they leave behind are real. Something is definitely seen. We just don't know what.

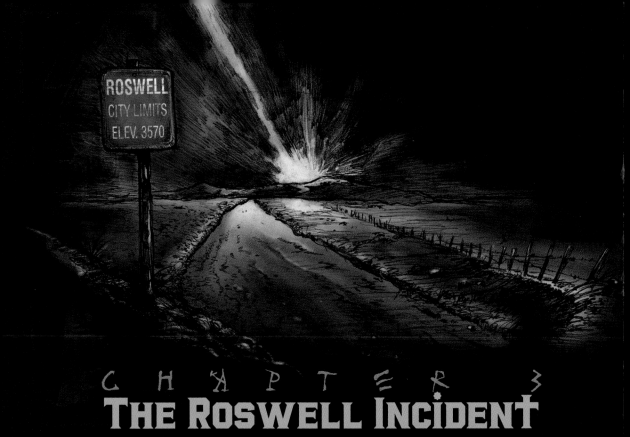

# CHAPTER 3
# THE ROSWELL INCIDENT

Without a doubt, the Roswell Incident is the most famous UFO case of all time. It occurred in 1947, one week after Kenneth Arnold's sighting. But just because it's famous doesn't mean it tells the true story of a crashed UFO. The only thing we know for sure is that something fell on Mac Brazel's ranch in Roswell, New Mexico, and smashed apart. The government said it was a weather balloon. Others insist it was a flying saucer carrying five little aliens. Will we ever find out what it really was?

The mythology around this incident is thick and deep. It has been accumulating for more than 50 years. Almost everyone from the original cast of characters has passed away, and the site has been swept clean of any bits of evidence it may have had. So the legend continues to grow.

Astronomer Carl Sagan
(left) believed that we
would one day discover life
in the universe, but he
seriously doubted that flying
saucers were evidence of it.

If anything, the Roswell Incident shows how badly we want to believe in aliens. It makes our hearts race faster and sends our imaginations on a great roller-coaster ride. But as astronomer Carl Sagan once said, "Extraordinary claims demand extraordinary proof." And this story makes some very extraordinary claims. This is what happened.

It is July 1, 1947. Strange blips start showing up on three different army radar screens. They move very fast and change direction suddenly. Nobody has the slightest idea what they are.

The following evening, a fierce thunderstorm tears apart the skies over Roswell, New Mexico. Dan Wilmot goes out on his front porch after dinner to watch the lightning show. The storm is fantastic. Between lightning flashes, Dan and his wife see something very bright streak across the sky. It falls toward the northeast and drops behind the horizon. Milkman Steve Robinson sees the same object. He describes it as bright, oval, and solid.

On July 3, Mac Brazel finds some kind of wreckage strewn over a large area of his ranch. He later told people that some of it was very shiny, like metal, but it was also very light. When he

## AREA 51

UFO buffs dream of making a pilgrimage to Area 51 in Nevada—not that they would ever be allowed in. Area 51 is a top secret military test site, where the so-called X-planes (short for "experimental planes") are assembled and flown. People living nearby report seeing strange lights zipping back and forth across the sky late at night, fueling the rumor that engineers were able to build a working model of the Roswell saucer.

Seven days after the crash in Roswell, New Mexico, the *Roswell Daily Record* ran a headline announcing that no details of the captured flying disk had been revealed.

tried crumpling it up, it just unfolded. It didn't dent when he pounded it with a sledgehammer. He also claimed to have seen strange symbols on several pieces of the debris.

Brazel called the army air base at Roswell to report the crash. Major Jesse Marcel immediately showed up with a team and began to clear away the wreckage. Then a very curious thing happened. The army issued a press release stating that it had captured a flying saucer.

Now, let's stop right here. The government had been doing its very best to play down the whole UFO thing. Flying saucers? Ridiculous! You saw clouds. You saw the lights on a blimp. You were dreaming. You were hallucinating. You were lying.

So why would the army tell the newspapers that a flying saucer had come down in New Mexico? It makes no sense. But let's go on.

Major Marcel's recovery team scooped up all the debris and brought it back to the base. It was then flown to Wright-Patterson Air Force Base in Ohio. Another press release was issued. The army had apparently changed its mind. It wasn't a flying saucer that crashed. It was a weather balloon. A weather balloon? Is that possible? Sure.

In the summer of 1947, the navy had begun launching enormous weather balloons under the name Operation Skyhook. The Skyhook balloons were teardrop shaped and made of a very thin plastic film. They carried an instrument pack high into the stratosphere to measure, among other things, cosmic rays.

The balloons had been developed in the General Mills research labs in Minneapolis, so everybody there knew all about them. But most people didn't. Even the folks in Minneapolis mistook the Skyhooks for UFOs. The balloons drifted so high up, you couldn't make out their shape. But

The army claimed the Roswell debris was really the wreckage of a downed weather balloon. This photograph shows a Skyhook balloon.

because they reflected sunlight, they looked like dancing spots of light. That made them the perfect UFO, except, of course, they weren't.

If you had seen one of these balloons lying on the ground, you'd certainly know what it was. But there was a terrible storm the night before the Roswell crash. All that wild weather could have easily brought down one of the balloons. The instrument pack would have been smashed to smithereens, and the balloon wouldn't have fared any better. So out goes Mac Brazel the next day and sees wreckage. It all looks unfamiliar to him. It is, in fact, very high tech. Brazel's a rancher, remember, not a scientist. He doesn't recognize the material. He sees symbols that he can't identify. But would you recognize these symbols?

$$\odot \quad \bullet \quad \equiv \quad \text{⌇} \quad \text{▲▲▲▲} \quad \infty \quad \text{⚡} \quad \text{ᚱ} \quad \text{Ƨ}$$

They certainly look like a strange language, but they're actually weather symbols. In fact, these symbols might very well have been on the Skyhook instrument packs. But would Brazel have known what they were? Did you know what they were?

## >> All This and Aliens Too.

There's more to this story, though. Over the years, dozens of people have been interviewed about the Roswell case, and some have made some pretty shocking claims. Here's a sample:

- They saw parts of the crashed saucer.
- They saw five dead aliens.

# ALIEN FLIGHT SCHOOL

Arguably, the most bizarre UFO story ever told comes
from the scientist Robert Lazar. Lazar claims that in 1987 he
was approached by naval intelligence and asked to work on a super
top secret project at Groom Lake, the site of Area 51. Lazar says he
spent about one year at a facility called S-4, trying to reconstruct one of
several alien saucers the government had apparently gotten its hands on.

Lazar, whose specialty is systems engineering, was told that UFOs use gravity
amplification—whatever that is—to get around and that they are partly fueled
by Element 115, a very heavy, radioactive metal that does not exist on Earth.

According to Lazar, the spacecraft he worked on was 35 feet in diameter
and had three levels. The middle level had seats for a crew of three
small aliens, and the lowest level housed the gravity amplifiers.
Lazar was not allowed to see the topmost level.

Lazar claims that this particular model was briefly test-flown.
It didn't get more than a few feet above the ground, but
its underside did give off a nifty blue glow.

· One of the aliens was still alive at the scene but later died.
· They watched the autopsy of the aliens.
· The saucer remains in a top secret location.

What are we to make of all this? Well, first we should remember what
Carl Sagan said. Extraordinary claims demand extraordinary proof.
So where's the proof?

A number of years ago, the Fox TV network aired a film that was
supposed to show the autopsy of one of the Roswell aliens. But

you would have to be awfully gullible to be taken in by this. The "autopsy" looked like something a bunch of college students would do for a prank. It was completely unprofessional, and the technique was all wrong. The "alien" was even worse. Yoda from the movie *Star Wars* was more realistic. The film wasn't very clear either, and there were, of course, no close-ups. A close-up would have shown the alien for what it most likely was—rubber. You also have to ask yourself why the film of a real alien autopsy wasn't classified super top secret. When the government wants to hide something, it does a very good job.

Okay. So maybe the autopsy was faked. But what about the people who claimed to have seen dead aliens? Without proof, all we have is their word—if it really is their word.

If you've ever played the game "telephone," you know how a message can change when it is passed from person to person. The Roswell Incident is over 50 years old. How many people have repeated the story? How many writers have used what others wrote as their source of information? Did all these people check their facts? And did these so-called eyewitnesses really exist in the first place, or are they just part of the mythology? If somebody is asking you to believe in aliens, the proof had better be good.

Until his death, Major Marcel insisted he had never seen anything like the Roswell wreckage. But Marcel was a staff intelligence officer. He had nothing to do with Operation Skyhook. So a downed balloon would have been just as unfamiliar to him as it was to Mac Brazel. But there's also another possibility. The crashed object could have been an experimental aircraft.

Roswell, New Mexico, is not far from the White Sands Missile Range. White Sands is not open to the public. Guess why. This is where the government tests its most secret missile and aircraft designs. But once the

Major Jesse Marcel poses with the remains of a tattered weather balloon.

aircraft are built, they have to be taken out and test-flown. So imagine a craft that's still experimental. All the bugs are not out of it yet. On a test flight, the pilot runs into trouble. The plane crashes during a severe thunderstorm, and the debris scatters over a large area. Mac Brazel finds it. "Wow!" he thinks. "What is *this*?"

The government now has a problem. Should they tell the public about this top secret aircraft? No way! So they announce that the army has captured a UFO. Then a couple of days later, they decide the UFO story may get way out of hand—which it did. So they change it. The wreckage becomes a weather balloon. It's not nearly as exciting as a crashed flying saucer packed with little aliens, but it's not as fantastic either.

In the world of UFOs, there are seekers of truth and dreamers of dreams. The truth lies somewhere among the Roswell wreckage, but it is hard to unearth. There have been too many dreamers along the way. So step carefully and remember what Carl Sagan said. If and when the aliens arrive, chances are, we'll know it.

# CHAPTER 4

# A UFO SAMPLER

Not everyone who reports a UFO actually sees a UFO. The sky is filled with many things that people simply don't recognize. The lights on advertising blimps. Unusual cloud formations. Meteors. Orbiting satellites. Venus. But there are times when a sighting cannot be so easily explained. Here are some of the cases that have truly baffled the investigators. Whatever these people saw remains a mystery.

This UFO photograph (facing page) was taken in Alabama in 1969.

# Case 1

Gujan-Mestras, France, June 19, 1978

t is 1:30 in the morning. Monsieur Bachère is driving west toward Bordeaux. As he approaches the town of La Réole, he sees a "large orange ball, very bright," hovering about 1,000 feet up in the night sky. Suddenly it disappears, only to reappear a minute later. Monsieur Bachère and his wife exchange looks and continue on their way.

n Gujan-Mestras, Monsieur Varisse is in his shop, baking fresh loaves of crusty bread for the morning. Perhaps he is whistling. Suddenly there is a knock at the door. Monsieur Varisse looks up. "Eh? Someone is here? At this hour?" He wipes his floury hands on his apron and crosses the room to see who it is.

Two teenagers are on the steps, shaking, terrified. They had pulled off the road, they tell him, to see if they could fix the broken turn signal in their car. Suddenly, all the streetlights went out, and they heard a powerful rumble. It sounded like an earthquake. They looked up and saw something red and oval about 1,000 feet up, heading straight for them.

Monsieur Varisse laughs. They are joking, of course. It is a teenage prank. He asks their names.

"Frank Pavia," says the one who looks a bit older.

The other boy is very upset. His eyes are red and moist.

33

"Jean-Marc," he stammers. "Jean-Marc Guitard."

This oval, they continue, was surrounded with white flames. Jean-Marc found it hard to breathe. Then he fainted. That's when the object changed direction and flew away. The boys are trembling.

Monsieur Varisse laughs again.

But when the boys' story reached the offices of GEPAN, the French center for UFO studies, nobody laughed. Others in the area had reported strange doings that night. So GEPAN decided to investigate.

Three scientists visited the site the following day. They interviewed the witnesses and brought them to the spot where they had seen the object. The witnesses described the object's color and movements and estimated its height above the ground. Soon additional witnesses started coming forward. A student who lived in Gujan-Mestras reported seeing orange flashes above the trees just as the streetlights went out. That had been about 12:30, he said. And he had heard a low rumble. The witnesses also agreed on the color of the object, as well as its size. But certainly the most interesting aspect was the UFO's power output, which had been enough

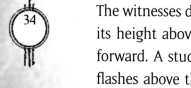

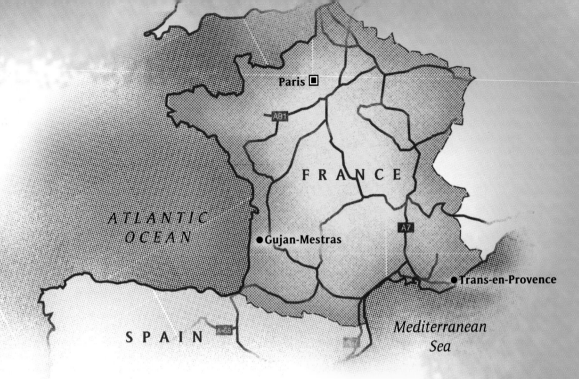

to trip the photoelectric cells in the streetlights. Conclusion: a very bright disk-shaped object with a diameter of about 16 feet had flown low over Gujan-Mestras, France, identity unknown.

## >> Case 2
### Trans-en-Provence, France, January 8, 1981

It is about 5:00 in the evening. Monsieur Nicolai is outside, building a concrete water pump behind his house. Suddenly, he hears "a faint whistling." He turns and sees "a device in the air," just about level with the top of a large pine tree. The object begins to descend. The whistling sound continues. Monsieur Nicolai moves closer. He would later recall that the object was not spinning, nor did he see any flames coming from it.

Monsieur Nicolai is about 30 yards away when he sees the device touch down. It remains on the ground for perhaps a second or two and then rises again. As it moves off, Monsieur Nicolai notices four openings on the underside of the object. He does not see any flames or smoke. The object heads northeast at a very high rate of speed, and in moments it is gone. A little while later, Monsieur Nicolai walks to the spot where the object landed and finds a circle about six feet in diameter. He also sees what looks like scratched areas here and there around the circle. The following morning, his wife and neighbor examine the circle. They urge Monsieur Nicolai to call the police.

About five weeks later, a team from GEPAN arrived to investigate the sighting. Soil and plant samples were taken, and Monsieur Nicolai was questioned several times. He reported that the object was shaped like "two saucers, one inverted on top of the other," ringed by a thick ridge. He described the object as being the color of lead. Underneath were four circles, which he compared to masonry pails.

There was an eight-foot retaining wall on the property, which helped Monsieur Nicolai estimate the size of the object. He figured the diameter to be about eight feet, and the height, no bigger than six feet.

Soil samples from the landing site were sent to a lab for analysis. Tests determined that the soil had been subjected to pressure and heat. Large, black particles found in the soil appeared to be combustion residue.

GEPAN was unable to draw any conclusions based on their investigations. The event remains unidentified.

## >> Case 3
### Irvine, California, August 3, 1965

It is just past noon. Rex Heflin, a highway maintenance engineer, pulls off the road to photograph a railroad crossing sign. Tree branches have grown over the sign, blocking it from view. It is Heflin's job to report this sort of thing to the county.

Heflin reaches for the Polaroid camera he always carries. He is just about to photograph the sign when he catches a flash of something out of the corner of his eye. Heflin is parked near the intersection of Myford Road and Walnut Avenue, about five miles from El Toro Marine Base.

## ROADSIDE UFOS

Travel America and you'll see how much we love our flying saucers. Not far from Austin, Texas, the Association for the Understanding of Man has set up an array of lights to help guide UFOs to a safe landing. There's another landing site in Pennsylvania. In Tennessee, Curtis King lives in a flying saucer-shaped house, and Al Thomas of Russellville, Arkansas, has a homemade flying saucer in a hangar behind his garage.

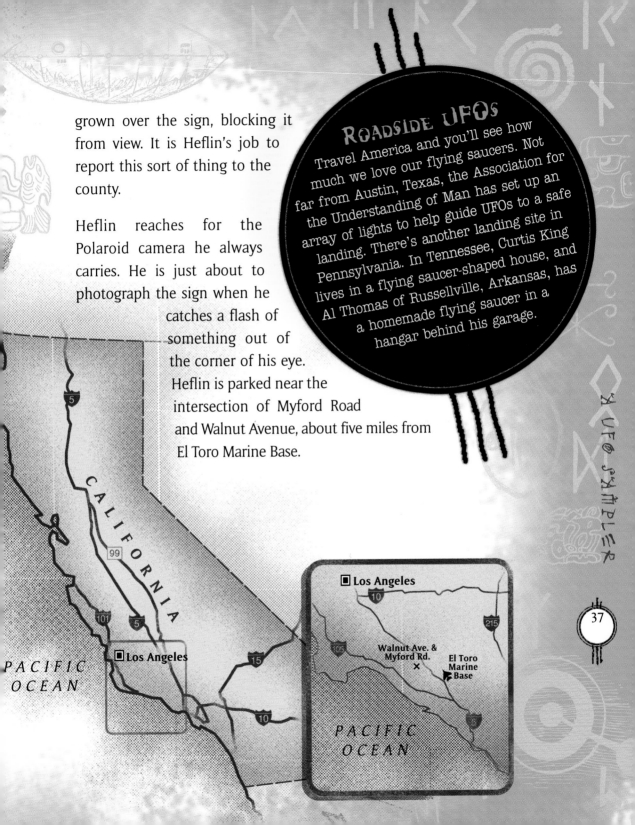

CALIFORNIA

5

99

101

5

Los Angeles

PACIFIC OCEAN

15

10

Los Angeles

10

105

Walnut Ave. & Myford Rd.

El Toro Marine Base

215

PACIFIC OCEAN

UFO SAMPLER

37

Rex Heflin used his Polaroid camera to photograph a UFO in flight over Southern California.

As the object approaches, Heflin can see that it is a silvery-colored craft of some sort. He assumes it's from the marine base. Something experimental, perhaps. As the craft crosses Myford Road, Heflin snaps a picture of it through the van's windshield. The craft continues eastward, tilting just enough to show a dark underside. That's when Heflin sees the beam of greenish-white light. It is coming from the very center of the craft, rotating clockwise, sweeping out a complete circle every two seconds. Heflin takes a second picture, this time through the passenger window.

At this point, the craft seems to wobble a little, as if it is losing stability. It begins to turn, and Heflin takes a third picture. The craft is still moving away. Heflin snaps a fourth and final picture as the object starts to climb, leaving what Heflin describes as a "smokelike vapor." Moments later, it shoots off and is swallowed up by the overcast. Heflin still thinks he has seen an experimental aircraft.

But here's where the story gets really interesting.

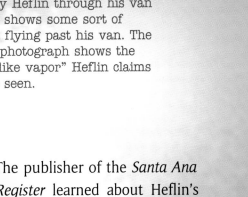

This series of photographs taken by Heflin through his van window shows some sort of aircraft flying past his van. The bottom photograph shows the "smokelike vapor" Heflin claims to have seen.

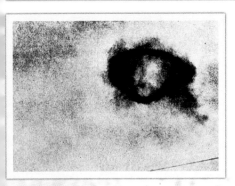

The publisher of the *Santa Ana Register* learned about Heflin's photos and eventually ran the story. As a result, marine corps intelligence officers showed up at Heflin's house. Then the air force got involved. Heflin was interviewed for more than three hours. Eventually, the sighting was labeled a hoax, even though the investigating officer's report stated that Heflin "*is not* attempting to perpetrate a hoax."

And then . . . on September 22, two men knocked on Heflin's door. They claimed to be from the North American Aerospace Defense Command (NORAD). They asked to borrow three of the four photographs. Heflin handed the pictures over, and that's the last he saw of the men. Their identity was never discovered. The object Heflin photographed remains unidentified.

## >> Case 4

### Mansfield, Ohio, October 18, 1973

This is known as the Coyne Helicopter Case, and it is about as intriguing as a UFO sighting can ever be. The witnesses were the four-man crew of an army reserve helicopter.

It is nearly 11:00 P.M. Sergeants John Healey and Robert Yanacsek, Lieutenant Arrigo Jezzi, and Captain Lawrence Coyne are on their way back to Cleveland. They are flying at an altitude of 2,500 feet. Their airspeed is 90 knots. All of a sudden Healey, who is in the left rear seat, spots a red light off to the west. It is heading south.

Just after 11:00 Yanacsek, in the right rear seat, sees a single red light on the eastern horizon. The light seems to be keeping pace with the helicopter. Yanacsek alerts Coyne, who tells him to "keep an eye on it." Thirty seconds later, the light begins closing in on the helicopter. Jezzi has been at the controls, but at this point Coyne takes over. He begins a powered descent, dropping 500 feet per minute. He contacts the Mansfield control tower and asks about jet traffic in the area. Before Mansfield can respond, all contact is lost.

Meanwhile, the red light continues to advance. It seems, in fact, to be heading straight for the helicopter.

"That thing must be doing over 600 knots!"

Coyne speeds up the helicopter's descent, but the light keeps coming. Then it slows and hangs there in front of the helicopter. Now Coyne, Healey, and Yanacsek can see that it is a gray, metallic, cigar-shaped object. And it is absolutely enormous. A red light is at the nose and a white light at the tail. A green beam spills from the underside. Rooted to their seats and speechless, the men watch as the beam sweeps across the windshield, bathing the interior in green light. There is no air turbulence and no noise. Coyne's hand is still on the altitude control, but instead of descending, the helicopter is climbing. It is now at 3,500 feet and moving higher at a rate of 1,000 feet per minute. The object hovers for a few more seconds and then suddenly shoots away.

Five ground witnesses confirmed the sighting. From their car, one adult and four children saw both the helicopter and the object. "It was a great big thing," said the oldest boy. "It lit up everything green." Despite a thorough investigation, the object encountered by the Coyne helicopter crew remains a mystery.

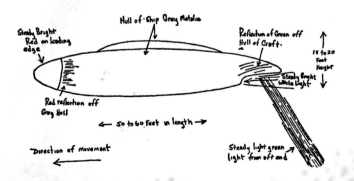

Steady Bright Red on leading edge

Hull of · Ship Grey Metalic

Reflection of Green off Hull of Craft.

15 to 20 Feet Height

Steady Bright White Light

Red reflection off Grey Hull

← 50 to 60 Feet in length →

Direction of movement

Steady light green light from aft end

An artist's interpretation of the UFO Captain Lawrence Coyne and his crew saw while flying over Ohio.

# SOMETHING IS SEEN . . . BUT WHAT IS IT?

We like to think we are very smart. We have peered into the heart of the atom. We have gazed outward through space. We can almost describe what conditions were like shortly after the big bang, the explosion that gave birth to the universe. But there are still so many things that we don't understand or even know about. UFOs are in this category.

Scientists with open minds are finding it harder and harder to deny the existence of UFOs. These things—whatever they are—leave traces. They scorch the ground. They crush the grass. They trip the photoelectric cells in streetlights. They show up on radar. And then they are gone, like a puff of smoke or a ghost. Like the images in a dream.

Lenticular (lens-shaped) clouds *(below and facing page)* are sometimes mistaken for UFOs.

Sometimes they seem to be under intelligent control. But if they are alien spacecraft, how can they just disappear? Where do they come from? Where do they go? Do they pop into another universe? Is there another universe?

There really aren't any theories—only suggestions. Here they are.

**UFOs are spaceships from another planet.** It's possible, of course, but it means accepting the following:

· Other planets that are favorable to life exist somewhere in the universe. (There is no proof of this yet.)
· The beings have somehow figured out where we are. (Earth circles a medium-sized star toward the edge of a galaxy filled with billions of stars. Basically, we're in the boondocks.)

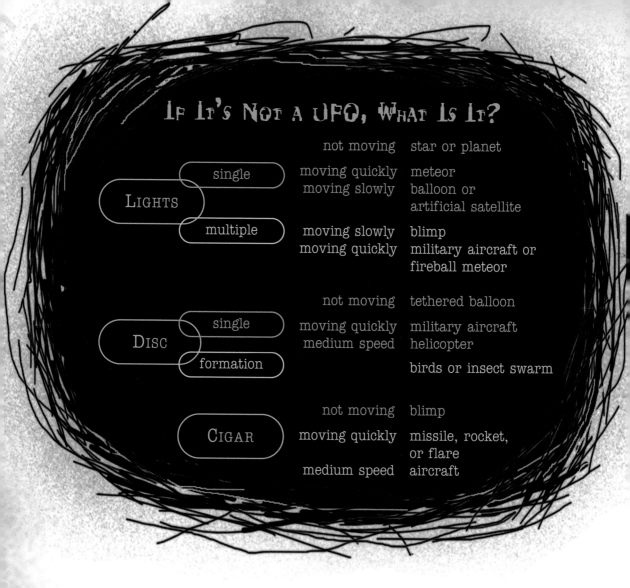

## If It's Not a UFO, What Is It?

| | | | |
|---|---|---|---|
| **LIGHTS** | single | not moving | star or planet |
| | | moving quickly | meteor |
| | | moving slowly | balloon or artificial satellite |
| | multiple | moving slowly | blimp |
| | | moving quickly | military aircraft or fireball meteor |
| **DISC** | single | not moving | tethered balloon |
| | | moving quickly | military aircraft |
| | | medium speed | helicopter |
| | formation | | birds or insect swarm |
| **CIGAR** | | not moving | blimp |
| | | moving quickly | missile, rocket, or flare |
| | | medium speed | aircraft |

· The ships are either remote controlled, or the aliens are very small. (Many UFOs seem to be no larger than the average bedroom. Those, of course, could be drone ships—ships without pilots.)

· The aliens are surveying us for some reason, or they just like scaring the pants off us.

That's an awful lot to swallow. Remember what Carl Sagan said.

**UFOs are holograms.** This is a very cool idea. A hologram, of course, is a three-dimensional image created by beams of light. So this would suggest that UFOs are essentially ghosts. The problem here, though, is that a hologram would not crush grass or leave burn marks.

**UFOs are warps in the fabric of space-time.** This is so weird that if UFOs turn out to be space-time warps, we still won't know what they are.

**UFOs are objects that exist alongside us but that we normally cannot perceive through our five senses.** Wow! What an amazing idea! And it's not as bizarre as it sounds.

Our five senses are good, but they don't pick up everything. Our eyes, for example, can see only a very narrow range of wavelengths. We can't see X rays, ultraviolet rays, microwaves, infrared rays, and a whole lot more. Our sense of smell is nowhere near that of a shark's. Dogs can hear frequencies that are way beyond us. So what makes us think we're getting the whole picture? There might be an awful lot of stuff going on around us that we don't know about. But maybe every so often, we catch a glimpse of it. An intriguing idea, to be sure.

And that, alas, is where we must leave it. For a very long time, few scientists considered UFOs worthy of study. They're beginning to change their minds, however. These things simply won't go away, and the evidence—although skimpy—suggests that *something* is going on. So keep your eyes on the sky, because just when you least expect it, who knows? You may just catch that glimpse. . . .

**Books//** Holmsten, Brian, and Alex Lubertozzi, eds. *The Complete War of the Worlds: Mars' Invasion of Earth from H. G. Wells to Orson Welles.* Naperville, IL: Sourcebooks, 2001. This book includes the complete texts of H. G. Wells's novel *The War of the Worlds* and the radio performance by *The Mercury Theatre on the Air.* The book is accompanied by two CDs that feature the entire original radio broadcast, a press conference given by Orson Welles the day after the broadcast, a variety of interviews, and more.

Kettelkamp, Larry. *ETs and UFOs: Are They Real?* New York: Morrow Junior Books, 1996. This book gives an overview of a variety of reported sightings of UFOs, including Kenneth Arnold's sighting and the Roswell Incident.

**Videos//** *Close Encounters of the Third Kind.* Writ. and dir. Steven Spielberg. Culver City, CA: Columbia/EMI, 1977. Videocassette. This motion picture depicts the arrival of flying saucers from an alien planet.

*Saucer Tech.* Vol. 3 of *UFOs and Aliens: Search for the Truth.* Narr. Jeri Ryan. Chicago: Questar, 2001. DVD. This videorecording examines the science of traveling beyond our solar system, including recent developments from NASA. It includes witness accounts of the Phoenix lights, a mass UFO sighting.

**We6sites//** *Pop Culture Mars* <http://mars.jpl.nasa.gov/mystique/history/index.html> This NASA website has a timeline of human observation of the planet Mars, from ancient times to the present.

*The Skeptiseum* <http://www.skeptiseum.org/exhibits/index.html> This virtual museum has images of artifacts and souvenirs related to topics such as UFOs and aliens, ghosts, ESP, and legendary creatures like Bigfoot and the Loch Ness Monster. The website is hosted by CSICOP, the Committee for the Scientific Investigation of Claims of the Paranormal.

47

## >> About the Author

Born in Baltimore, Maryland, Judith Herbst grew up in Queens, New York, where she learned to jump double Dutch with amazing skill. She has since lost that ability. A former English teacher, she ran away from school in her tenure year to become a writer. Her first book for kids was *Sky Above and Worlds Beyond,* whose title, she admits, was much too long. She loves to write and would rather be published, she says, than be rich, which has turned out to be the case. Herbst spends summers in Maine on a lake with her cats and laptop.

## >> Photo Acknowledgments

Photographs and illustrations in this book are used with the permission of: © Christel Gerstenberg/CORBIS, p. 6; Fortean Picture Library, pp. 7, 9, 11, 12, 14, 15, 18, 19, 20, 26, 27, 31, 32, 38, 39 (all), 41, 42, 43; © Bettmann/CORBIS, p. 8; Hollywood Book and Poster, p. 10; Llewellyn Publications/Fortean Picture Library, p. 16; August C. Roberts/ Fortean Picture Library, p. 23; AP/Wide World Photos, p. 25. Maps and illustrations by Bill Hauser, pp. 4–5, 25, 33, 34, 35, 37, 40.

Cover image by Fortean Picture Library.